Raise of brain : exploring the shrewdness

Written by Madhav Bansal

An Artificial Intelligence work
Concept / Prompt Writer : Madhav Bansal

PREFACE

Welcome to the exploration of artificial intelligence, a journey through the intricate landscapes of innovation and ethical contemplation. In these pages, we embark on a quest to understand the profound impact of AI on our world—its promises, its challenges, and the intricate dance between human ingenuity and machine intelligence.

As we delve into the realms of AI, it becomes evident that this technology is not merely a tool; it's a transformative force reshaping industries, societies, and the very fabric of our daily lives. The chapters that follow are a tapestry woven with threads of curiosity, caution, and a relentless pursuit of understanding.

Our odyssey begins with an examination of the unparalleled advancements AI brings to fields like healthcare, finance, and education. We unravel the potential for AI to augment human capabilities, fostering a synergy that transcends conventional boundaries. Yet, as with any transformative power, there lie shadows that demand our attention.

The chapters dedicated to the cons of AI unravel the complexities embedded in its rise. From job displacement concerns to ethical dilemmas, we confront the darker side of technological progress. It is a call to awareness, urging us to navigate this frontier with eyes wide open and a commitment to responsible innovation.

The chapter titles themselves reflect the dichotomy of AI's influence—"Rise of the Machines," "Ethics in the Algorithm," and "Echoes of Tomorrow." Each title echoes the nuances of a landscape where possibilities and perils coexist, challenging us to ponder, question, and envision a future shaped by both human wisdom and artificial intelligence.

In the quest for balance, we add brushstrokes to our canvas—exploring AI's role in creativity, from generative art to AI-driven music composition. This narrative extends beyond technology, touching the very essence of what it means to create, innovate, and collaborate in a world where machines are our companions in the creative process.

As we navigate the chapters of this book, I invite you to join me in a reflection on the dual nature of AI. It is a force that propels us forward into uncharted territories, accompanied by the responsibility to safeguard our humanity. This book is an invitation to explore, learn, and engage in the ongoing dialogue that shapes the future of artificial intelligence.

May this exploration spark curiosity, kindle contemplation, and inspire a collective journey into the boundless possibilities and ethical considerations woven into the intricate tapestry of AI. We also explore Q&A session with AI. All Data and Theory from starter to End given by AI , Hope you enjoyed the journey of **World of Automation Brain.**

Welcome to the frontier.

Madhav Bansal

Chapters :

- **The Rise of Silicon Minds**
    Unveiling the Emergence of Artificial Intelligence
- **Byte-sized Brilliance**
    Exploring the Pros of AI Intelligence
- **Digital Paradox: Navigating the Digital Morality**
    Code of Ethics: Navigating the Moral Compass in AI
- **Algorithmic Alchemy**
    Discovering the shrewdness of Algorithmic
- **Minds and Machines: A Symbiotic Dance**
    Examining the Interplay Between Humans and AI
- **Coalescence : Human -AI Fusion**
    Ethical Quandaries: Navigating the MoralLandscape
- **Rules for the Unseen: Governing AI Futures**
    AI and the Surveillance Dilemma
- **Bio-Bots: AI in the Realm of Biology**
    Revolutionising Healthcare and Biotechnology
- **Privacy Paradox: Navigating the Digital Maze**
    Addressing Security and Privacy Challenges
- **Nyctophobia**
    Dark Corners: Risks and Security Challenges
- **Encoding- Decoding of Emotional Error**
    Human-Machine Collaboration: A New Frontier
- **The Road Ahead !**
    The Road Ahead: AI Trends and Future Frontiers
- **Echoes of Tomorrow**
    Echoes of Sci-Fi Inspirations and AI Realities
- **The shadows of Displacement**
  The Shadow of Unemployment: AI and Job Displacement
- **Dystopian Eye**
    Data Dystopia: Privacy Erosion in the AI Era

"The Rise of Sillicon Minds"

Chapter 1 - The Rise of Silicon Minds

C ognitive Architects: The Minds Behind AI
Development"
In the annals of technological history, a select
group of visionaries has shaped the landscape of
artificial intelligence. This chapter embarks on a journey
through time, exploring the profound contributions of
individuals who laid the foundation for the rise of
intelligent machines.

The Visionaries
The story begins with the groundbreaking work of Alan
Turing, often regarded as the father of computer science.
Turing's theoretical framework for computation and the
famous Turing Test provided early glimpses into the
possibilities of artificial thought. As we traverse through
the decades, the narrative unveils the brilliance of
pioneers like John McCarthy, Marvin Minsky, and
Herbert A. Simon, who founded the field of artificial
intelligence in the 1950s.
From Laboratories to Silicon Valley:
The chapter unfolds the evolution of AI research from
academic laboratories to the tech epicentre
of Silicon Valley. Stanford University emerges as a
pivotal hub, nurturing talents such as John McCarthy
and fostering the birth of AI laboratories that would go
on to become Silicon Valley giants.

The Cognitive Revolution
As we navigate the cognitive revolution of the 1980s, the chapter illuminates the paradigm shift from rule-based systems to neural networks. The contributions of Geoffrey Hinton, Yoshua Bengio, and Yann LeCun come to the forefront as their work forms the backbone of modern machine learning, particularly deep learning.

Interdisciplinary Symphony
An essential aspect explored is the interdisciplinary nature of AI development. Computer scientists collaborate with neuroscientists, linguists, and experts from diverse fields to unravel the intricacies of mimicking human intelligence. The chapter emphasises the symbiotic relationship between various disciplines, creating a tapestry of knowledge essential for AI advancement.

"Byte-sized Brilliance"

Chapter 2: "Byte-sized Brilliance: Understanding Machine Learning"

Machine learning, the driving force behind contemporary artificial intelligence, takes center stage in this chapter. We embark on a journey through the intricate world of algorithms, data, and the transformative power of machines to learn and adapt.

Foundations of Machine Learning
The chapter kicks off by demystifying the fundamentals of machine learning, breaking down complex concepts for readers unfamiliar with technical jargon. It elucidates how machines, devoid of explicit programming, can learn from data and improve their performance over time.

Types of Machine Learning Algorithms
Readers are guided through the diverse landscape of machine learning algorithms. From supervised learning, where models are trained on labeled data, to unsupervised learning, where algorithms uncover patterns in unlabelled data, the chapter provides a comprehensive overview. Reinforcement learning, with its roots in behavioural psychology, is explored as a paradigm where algorithms learn through trial and error.

Real-world Applications
To illustrate the practical impact of machine learning, the narrative seamlessly transitions to real-world

applications. Examples span various domains, from predicting stock market trends and optimising supply chains to enhancing healthcare diagnostics. Through compelling case studies, readers witness the tangible benefits of machine learning in solving complex problems.

Ethical Considerations
As the chapter progresses, it doesn't shy away from the ethical dimensions of machine learning. The discussion touches upon algorithmic bias, transparency issues, and the potential consequences of unchecked automation. By highlighting both the positive and challenging aspects, readers gain a nuanced understanding of the ethical landscape surrounding machine learning.

"Digital Paradox: Navigating the Digital Morality "

Chapter 3: "Code of Ethics: Navigating the Moral Compass in AI"

As artificial intelligence continues to permeate our lives, this chapter navigates the complex terrain of ethics in AI development and deployment. It explores the moral dimensions that arise when machines start making decisions and the responsibility that accompanies such advancements.

The Moral Imperative
The chapter begins by emphasising the moral imperative in AI, drawing parallels with historical ethical considerations in technological progress. It explores the profound impact of AI on society and the need for a robust ethical framework to guide its development.

Unraveling Bias
One of the central themes of the chapter revolves around the challenge of algorithmic bias. Readers are taken on a journey through real-world examples where AI systems have inadvertently perpetuated or amplified societal biases. The discussion underscores the importance of addressing bias to ensure fairness and equity in AI applications.

Transparency and Accountability
To build trust in AI systems, the narrative delves into the critical aspects of transparency and accountability. It

explores the challenges of understanding complex algorithms and advocates for transparency in AI decision-making processes. The chapter also discusses mechanisms for holding developers and organisations accountable for the outcomes of AI systems.

The Quest for Ethical Guidelines
As the chapter unfolds, it explores ongoing efforts to establish ethical guidelines within the AI community. Initiatives by organisations, researchers, and industry leaders are highlighted, showcasing a collective commitment to aligning AI advancements with societal values.

"Algorithmic Alchemy"

Chapter 4: "Algorithm Alley: Decoding the Language of Machines"

This chapter embarks on a journey into the intricate world of algorithms, the unsung heroes shaping the behaviour of artificial intelligence. As readers navigate through Algorithm Alley, they gain a deeper understanding of the language of machines and the profound impact algorithms have on our daily lives.

Demystifying Algorithms

The chapter begins by demystifying the concept of algorithms, breaking down complex processes into digestible insights. It explores how algorithms serve as sets of instructions that guide machines, making decisions, solving problems, and learning from data.

Online Experience and Decision-Making

As readers traverse Algorithm Alley, they discover how algorithms shape their online experiences. From personalised recommendations on streaming platforms to targeted advertising on social media, the narrative illustrates the pervasive role of algorithms in tailoring content and services to individual preferences.

The Power and Pitfalls

To provide a balanced perspective, the chapter delves into the power and pitfalls of algorithms. It highlights the efficiency and accuracy they bring to various domains, such as healthcare diagnostics and financial predictions. Simultaneously, it explores the challenges, including the risk of perpetuating biases and the unintended consequences of algorithmic decision-making.

Transparency in Algorithmic Processes
Recognising the importance of transparency, the narrative explores the call for greater clarity in algorithmic processes. It discusses the challenges of understanding complex algorithms and advocates for mechanisms that ensure transparency in how decisions are made, particularly in applications with significant societal impact.

"Minds and Machines: A Symbiotic Dance "

Chapter 5: "Machines Among Us: AI in Everyday Life"

This chapter immerses readers in the pervasive presence of artificial intelligence in our daily lives. From the mundane to the extraordinary, the narrative explores how AI seamlessly integrates into various aspects of society, transforming the way we work, communicate, and navigate the world.

The Everyday AI Experience

The journey begins with a snapshot of the everyday AI experience, from voice-activated assistants managing our schedules to smart home devices anticipating our needs. Readers are invited to reflect on the subtle yet profound ways AI has become an integral part of modern living.

AI in the Workplace

The chapter then shifts its focus to the workplace, where AI-driven tools and systems enhance productivity and decision-making. From automating routine tasks to aiding complex problem-solving, the narrative highlights the symbiotic relationship between human workers and intelligent machines, dispelling fears of job displacement with a nuanced perspective.

Communication Revolution

Readers are then immersed in the communication revolution sparked by AI. Social media algorithms curate personalised content, chatbots facilitate customer service, and language translation tools bridge global communication gaps. The chapter explores how AI is not only a tool but a catalyst for transforming how we connect and share information.

Navigating AI Ethics in Everyday Life

Acknowledging the omnipresence of AI, the narrative weaves through the ethical considerations embedded in our AI-driven interactions. From privacy concerns to the impact on social dynamics, readers are prompted to contemplate the evolving ethical landscape and their role as informed participants in the AI-infused society.

"Coalescence: Human-AI Fusion"

Chapter 6: "Ethical Quandaries: Navigating the Moral Landscape"

This chapter delves deep into the ethical challenges posed by the rise of artificial intelligence. As society entrusts machines with increasingly complex decision-making, a myriad of moral questions emerge, and this chapter seeks to unravel the intricate threads of the ethical landscape in the realm of AI.

The Moral Fabric of AI
The narrative begins by examining the moral underpinnings of AI, emphasising the responsibility that comes with creating intelligent systems. It explores the fundamental question of whether machines should be programmed to emulate human morality and the implications of the choices made in defining ethical parameters.

Bias and Fairness
A significant portion of the chapter is dedicated to unraveling the ethical dimensions of bias in AI algorithms. Readers are guided through real-world instances where biased algorithms have perpetuated discrimination. The discussion extends to the ongoing efforts within the AI community to mitigate bias and foster fairness in algorithmic decision-making.

Accountability and Transparency
The narrative then navigates the complex terrain of accountability and transparency. It explores the challenges of assigning responsibility when AI systems make consequential decisions. The call for transparency is underscored, advocating for open dialogue and visibility into the inner workings of algorithms to foster trust and accountability.

Ethical Frameworks and Guidelines
Recognising the need for a guiding moral compass, the chapter explores existing ethical frameworks and guidelines in the development and deployment of AI. From industry-led initiatives to interdisciplinary collaborations, readers gain insights into the evolving efforts to establish ethical standards that align with societal values.

"Rules for the Unseen: Governing AI Futures"

Chapter 7: "AI and the Surveillance Dilemma"

This chapter delves into the intricate relationship between artificial intelligence and the ever-evolving landscape of privacy. As AI systems become more sophisticated and pervasive, the chapter navigates the delicate balance between innovation and the protection of personal privacy.

The Digital Panopticon
The narrative begins by examining the concept of a "digital panopticon," where AI-driven surveillance technologies have the potential to monitor and analyze individuals on an unprecedented scale. Readers are introduced to real-world examples, from facial recognition in public spaces to data collection through smart devices, illuminating the scope of the surveillance dilemma.

Trade-offs and Benefits
As the chapter unfolds, it explores the inherent trade-offs between privacy and the benefits derived from AI applications. From personalised recommendations to enhanced security measures, readers are prompted to consider the dual nature of AI's impact on our lives and the choices we make regarding the information we willingly share.

Legal and Ethical Considerations

Navigating the complex legal and ethical considerations, the narrative examines the current regulatory landscape surrounding privacy in the context of AI. It explores landmark privacy laws, such as GDPR, and discusses the challenges in adapting legal frameworks to address the rapid advancements in AI technology.

Empowering Users

Recognising the agency of individuals in the privacy equation, the chapter explores the role of user empowerment. It discusses tools and initiatives that empower individuals to understand and control how their data is used, fostering a sense of autonomy in an age of increasing digital interconnectedness.

"Bio-Bots: AI in the Realm of Biology"

Chapter 8: "The Promise of Progress: AI in Medicine and Science"

This chapter embarks on a journey through the transformative impact of artificial intelligence on the fields of medicine and science. From revolutionising diagnostics to unlocking new frontiers in research, the narrative illuminates the promises and challenges that AI brings to the realms of healthcare and scientific exploration.

Diagnostic Revolution

The chapter begins by delving into the diagnostic revolution brought about by AI in medicine. Readers are introduced to AI-powered diagnostic tools that analyze medical images, interpret test results, and assist healthcare professionals in making accurate and timely diagnoses. Real-world success stories highlight the potential for AI to enhance medical decision-making.

Personalised Medicine

Navigating through the landscape of personalised medicine, the narrative explores how AI tailors treatments to individual patients. From genomic analysis to predicting disease risks, readers gain insights into how AI is reshaping the approach to healthcare, offering targeted and effective interventions based on individual characteristics.

Drug Discovery and Research
The chapter extends its focus to the realm of scientific research, showcasing how AI accelerates drug discovery and advances scientific knowledge. From identifying potential drug candidates to analysing vast datasets for research insights, the narrative emphasises the collaborative synergy between AI and human researchers.

Ethical Considerations in Healthcare
Recognising the transformative potential of AI in healthcare, the narrative turns its attention to the ethical considerations inherent in these advancements. Discussions revolve around patient privacy, the responsible use of sensitive health data, and the need for ethical frameworks that guide the integration of AI technologies into healthcare practices.

"Nyctophobia"

Chapter 9: "Dark Corners: Risks and Security Challenges"

This chapter delves into the shadowy realms of risks and security challenges accompanying the rapid proliferation of artificial intelligence. As AI becomes more integrated into critical systems and infrastructure, the narrative navigates through the potential threats and vulnerabilities that demand careful consideration.

Threat Landscape
The chapter begins by painting a comprehensive picture of the evolving threat landscape associated with AI. From adversarial attacks on machine learning models to the exploitation of vulnerabilities in AI-powered systems, readers are immersed in the multifaceted challenges that emerge as technology advances.

Security in AI Systems
As the narrative unfolds, it explores the critical importance of security in AI systems. The discussion encompasses securing data used to train models, safeguarding the integrity of algorithms, and fortifying the deployment of AI in various applications. Real-world examples highlight the potential consequences of inadequate security measures.

Ethical Hacking and AI
Acknowledging the proactive stance against potential threats, the chapter examines the role of ethical hacking

in identifying vulnerabilities in AI systems. It delves into the ethical considerations of ethical hacking, emphasising the collaborative efforts between security experts and AI developers to fortify systems against malicious intent.

Future-proofing Against Risks
The narrative concludes by addressing strategies to future-proof AI against risks. It explores the ongoing research and development in creating robust, secure AI systems. The chapter prompts readers to contemplate the collective responsibility in ensuring the responsible development and deployment of AI technologies to mitigate potential risks.

"Encoding- Decoding of Emotional Error"

Chapter 10: "Human-Machine Collaboration: A New Frontier"

This chapter immerses readers in the evolving landscape of human-machine collaboration, where the synergy between humans and artificial intelligence opens new frontiers in innovation and problem-solving. The narrative explores the symbiotic relationship between human intelligence and machine capabilities, ushering in a new era of collaborative potential.

Augmented Intelligence
The chapter begins by introducing the concept of augmented intelligence, emphasising the enhancement of human capabilities through AI. Readers delve into scenarios where AI acts as a collaborator, providing insights, automating repetitive tasks, and augmenting human decision-making across various domains, from business to creative endeavours.

Cognitive Diversity
Navigating through the realm of human-machine collaboration, the narrative emphasises the significance of cognitive diversity. It explores how AI systems, with their unique problem-solving approaches, complement human perspectives, fostering a more comprehensive and innovative decision-making process.

Creative Partnerships

The chapter extends its focus to creative partnerships between humans and AI. Readers are immersed in examples where AI algorithms contribute to artistic endeavours, music composition, and other creative fields. The narrative challenges preconceived notions about the boundaries of creativity in the age of intelligent machines.

Challenges and Opportunities

As the narrative unfolds, it doesn't shy away from addressing the challenges associated with human-machine collaboration. Ethical considerations, potential job displacement, and the need for clear communication between humans and machines are explored. Simultaneously, the chapter underscores the vast opportunities for innovation and progress in this collaborative frontier.

"The Road Ahead ! "

Chapter 11: "The Road Ahead: AI Trends and Future Frontiers"

This chapter serves as a compass, guiding readers through the current trends and future frontiers of artificial intelligence. It illuminates the trajectory of AI advancements, emerging technologies, and the potential societal impacts that await on the horizon.

Evolution of AI Trends
The narrative begins by tracing the evolution of AI trends, from the early stages of rule-based systems to the current era dominated by machine learning and neural networks. Readers witness the dynamic nature of AI research and development, exploring key milestones that have shaped the field.

AI in Edge Computing and IoT
As the chapter unfolds, it delves into the intersection of AI with edge computing and the Internet of Things (IoT). The narrative explores how AI's integration with edge devices transforms real-time processing, enabling applications ranging from smart cities to autonomous vehicles.

Quantum Computing and AI
Navigating through the cutting edge, the chapter addresses the synergy between quantum computing and AI. Readers are introduced to the potential breakthroughs that quantum computing can bring to

machine learning algorithms, unlocking new dimensions of processing power and problem-solving capabilities.

Ethical Considerations in Future AI
Anticipating the future, the chapter dedicates space to ethical considerations in the development and deployment of advanced AI technologies. It prompts readers to contemplate the responsible integration of AI in emerging applications and the importance of aligning progress with ethical frameworks.

"Echoes of Tomorrow"

Chapter 12: "Echoes of Tomorrow: Sci-Fi Inspirations and AI Realities"

This concluding chapter delves into the intriguing relationship between science fiction visions of artificial intelligence and the tangible realities that have emerged in the AI landscape. It invites readers to reflect on how the imaginative narratives of the past have influenced, inspired, and sometimes forewarned about the present and future of AI.

Sci-Fi Visions and Reality

The narrative begins by examining classic and contemporary science fiction portrayals of AI, from Isaac Asimov's robotic laws to the sentient machines of recent cinematic narratives. Readers embark on a journey to explore the commonalities and divergences between these imaginative constructs and the actual technological advancements we witness today.

Impact on Popular Culture

As the chapter unfolds, it delves into the profound impact of AI on popular culture. From iconic AI characters in literature and movies to the influence of AI-themed storytelling on societal perceptions, readers gain insights into how fictional narratives have shaped public understanding and expectations surrounding intelligent machines.

Lessons from Sci-Fi:
The narrative goes beyond mere exploration, encouraging readers to extract valuable lessons from sci-fi visions. It prompts contemplation on the ethical dilemmas presented in fictional AI scenarios, the unintended consequences depicted in narratives, and the wisdom that can be gleaned from both utopian and dystopian perspectives.

The Role of Imagination
Concluding the journey, the chapter emphasises the enduring power of human imagination in shaping the trajectory of technological progress. It prompts readers to consider the responsibility that comes with envisioning and building AI systems, acknowledging the influence of creative visions in steering the development and societal integration of intelligent machines.

"The Shadow of Displacement"

Chapter 13: "The Shadow of Unemployment: AI and Job Displacement"

In an era dominated by technological advancements, the shadow of unemployment looms large as artificial intelligence (AI) continues to reshape the employment landscape. The rapid integration of AI technologies has brought about unprecedented efficiency gains but not without consequences for the workforce.

As automation becomes more prevalent, certain jobs are at risk of displacement, raising concerns about the future of work. Industries that heavily rely on routine, repetitive tasks are particularly vulnerable. Manufacturing, customer service, and even aspects of white-collar professions face the encroaching influence of AI.

The promise of increased productivity and cost savings is a double-edged sword, as it comes at the expense of jobs traditionally performed by humans. Machines equipped with advanced algorithms can execute tasks at a speed and precision unmatched by their human counterparts. While this heralds progress, it simultaneously raises questions about the fate of those left in the wake of automation.

The impact of AI on employment is not uniform across sectors. While some industries witness a surge in demand for skilled professionals to develop, maintain, and manage AI systems, others experience a decline in demand for routine tasks that AI can efficiently handle. This dichotomy exacerbates existing economic inequalities, creating a divide between those equipped with the skills to navigate the digital landscape and those left behind.

Addressing the challenges posed by AI-driven unemployment requires a multifaceted approach. Education and training programs must adapt to equip the workforce with the skills needed in an AI-driven economy. Governments and businesses alike must invest in re-Skilling initiatives to ensure that workers are not left obsolete by the relentless march of technology.

Furthermore, fostering an environment that encourages collaboration between humans and AI is essential. AI should be viewed as a tool that complements human capabilities rather than a replacement. Emphasising creativity, emotional intelligence, and critical thinking—qualities that AI lacks—can pave the way for a more harmonious integration of technology and human labor.

Policy interventions are crucial to mitigating the negative effects of AI-driven unemployment. Governments must enact measures to support displaced workers, offering retraining programs, unemployment benefits, and policies that promote the creation of new job opportunities in emerging industries.

The shadow of unemployment cast by AI is not inevitable doom but a call to action. Embracing the potential of AI while actively addressing its socioeconomic repercussions is key to shaping a future where technology serves humanity without leaving individuals in the dark. Balancing progress with inclusivity is the challenge of our time, and meeting it head-on requires collective efforts from policymakers, businesses, and society as a whole.

Chapter 14: "Data Dystopia: Privacy Erosion in the AI Era"

In the ever-expanding realm of artificial intelligence (AI), the erosion of privacy has emerged as a pressing concern, giving rise to what can be described as a "Data Dystopia." As AI technologies evolve and proliferate, the vast amounts of data they rely on become valuable commodities, raising critical questions about the ethical implications of our digital existence.

The foundation of many AI systems rests on the collection and analysis of personal data. From online behaviours and preferences to biometric information, individuals generate a constant stream of data that feeds the algorithms driving AI applications. While this data is instrumental in enhancing AI capabilities, it comes at a cost— the erosion of privacy.

Tech giants and other entities amass colossal datasets, often without clear transparency or user consent. This accumulation of personal information poses inherent risks, as it opens the door to potential misuse and abuse. The dystopian aspect lies in the imbalance of power, where individuals unknowingly relinquish control over their digital lives, becoming subjects of constant surveillance.

Machine learning algorithms, central to many AI systems, thrive on patterns and insights derived from vast datasets. However, the flip side of this capability is the potential for invasive profiling and the manipulation of individuals through targeted content delivery. In the Data Dystopia, personalised advertisements transform into a sophisticated tool for influencing opinions and behaviours, challenging the very fabric of democratic discourse.

The convergence of AI and surveillance technologies further amplifies privacy concerns. Facial recognition, predictive policing, and smart city initiatives blur the lines between public and private spaces, creating an environment where individuals feel perpetually monitored. This erosion of anonymity raises fundamental questions about the right to privacy in an era dominated by AI-driven surveillance.

As society grapples with the ramifications of Data Dystopia, there is an urgent need for robust privacy regulations and ethical frameworks. Striking a balance between technological innovation and safeguarding individual rights requires proactive measures from governments, industry leaders, and the wider public. Transparency in data practices, informed consent, and stringent regulations are essential to curbing the excesses of data collection and usage.

Individuals, too, play a pivotal role in navigating the challenges of privacy erosion. Educating the public about the risks associated with AI technologies and empowering them to make informed choices about data sharing are crucial steps in preserving individual autonomy in the digital age.

The road ahead involves a collective effort to steer the trajectory of AI towards a future that upholds privacy as a fundamental human right. By addressing the ethical dimensions of data usage and advocating for responsible AI practices, society can strive to prevent the descent into a full-fledged Data Dystopia, ensuring that the benefits of AI are realised without sacrificing the essence of personal privacy.

"Fairness and Ethical Conundrum"

Chapter 15: "The Bias Conundrum: Addressing Ethical Quagmires in AI"

In the age of artificial intelligence (AI), the pervasive issue of bias has become a formidable conundrum, casting a shadow over the ethical landscape of AI development and deployment. As AI systems increasingly influence decision-making processes across various domains, the inadvertent perpetuation of biases raises critical questions about fairness, accountability, and the societal impact of these advanced technologies.

The roots of bias in AI can be traced back to the data on which these systems are trained. Machine learning algorithms learn from historical data, inheriting the biases present in that data. Whether it be biased hiring practices, historical inequalities, or systemic prejudices, AI systems can unwittingly amplify and perpetuate these biases, creating a ripple effect that extends into various aspects of society.

The ethical quagmire lies in the unintended consequences of biased AI. From biased facial recognition systems disproportionately affecting certain demographics to AI-driven hiring tools reinforcing gender and racial biases, the ramifications are far-reaching. The reinforcement of societal prejudices through seemingly impartial algorithms challenges the principles of justice and equality that underpin ethical decision-making.

Addressing the bias conundrum demands a multi-faceted approach. Transparency in AI systems is paramount—developers must openly acknowledge the potential biases within their algorithms. Moreover, diverse and inclusive representation in the teams designing and implementing AI systems can help mitigate the risk of unintentional biases and bring a variety of perspectives to the table.

Continuous monitoring and auditing of AI systems are essential to identify and rectify biases as they emerge. This involves not only assessing the algorithms themselves but also scrutinising the data inputs and outputs to ensure fairness. Additionally, incorporating ethical considerations into the design phase, known as "ethical AI by design," can help embed fairness and accountability into the very fabric of AI development.

Governments and regulatory bodies play a pivotal role in navigating the bias conundrum. Establishing clear guidelines and regulations for ethical AI practices can provide a framework for developers and organisations to follow. As AI systems become increasingly integrated into society, responsible governance becomes crucial to prevent discriminatory outcomes and protect the rights of individuals.

Ultimately, the path forward involves a collective commitment to ethical AI. Industry stakeholders, policymakers, and the broader public must engage in an ongoing dialogue to navigate the complexities of bias in AI. By fostering an ethical mindset, prioritizing transparency, and embracing diversity in AI development, we can strive to create a future where AI technologies enhance human well-being without perpetuating and exacerbating societal biases.

"AI Vulnerabilities"

Chapter 16: "Security Breaches and AI Vulnerabilities"

The integration of artificial intelligence (AI) into our technological landscape brings unprecedented capabilities but also introduces new frontiers of concern, prominently among them being security breaches and vulnerabilities. As AI systems become more sophisticated, so do the potential risks associated with their misuse, posing a significant challenge to the security landscape.

One of the primary concerns revolves around adversarial attacks on AI systems. These attacks involve manipulating input data to mislead the AI model's decision-making process. Whether in image recognition, natural language processing, or other applications, adversaries can exploit vulnerabilities in the AI algorithms to force incorrect or unintended outputs. This poses a tangible threat, especially in critical areas such as autonomous vehicles, healthcare diagnostics, and cybersecurity.

The interconnected nature of AI systems also magnifies the impact of security breaches. A compromise in one part of an AI ecosystem can have cascading effects, leading to broader vulnerabilities. For instance, if an attacker gains unauthorized access to the training data or model parameters, it could compromise the integrity of the entire AI system, potentially resulting in biased decisions or manipulation of outcomes.

The increasing reliance on AI for decision-making in sensitive domains, including finance, healthcare, and national security, amplifies the potential consequences of security breaches. Malicious actors may exploit vulnerabilities to manipulate AI-driven systems, leading to financial fraud, compromised patient data, or even the manipulation of geopolitical events.

Addressing AI vulnerabilities requires a proactive and comprehensive approach. Regular security audits and testing of AI systems are crucial to identifying and patching vulnerabilities. Additionally, developers must implement robust encryption and access controls to safeguard sensitive data and prevent unauthorized manipulation of AI models.

As the AI landscape evolves, collaboration among industry stakeholders, researchers, and policymakers is essential. Establishing standardized security protocols and best practices for AI development can create a collective defense against emerging threats. Furthermore, ongoing research into AI security, including the development of secure-by-design algorithms, is crucial to stay ahead of evolving cyber threats.

Regulatory frameworks also play a pivotal role in ensuring AI security. Governments and international bodies need to enact and enforce regulations that mandate stringent security measures for AI systems.

This includes transparency requirements regarding how AI systems are secured, regular audits, and consequences for entities that fail to adhere to established security standards.

In the dynamic interplay between technological innovation and cybersecurity, addressing AI vulnerabilities is an ongoing process. By fostering a culture of security awareness, promoting collaboration, and staying vigilant against emerging threats, we can navigate the complex landscape of AI security and harness the potential of AI technologies responsibly.

"The Canvas of Creativity"

Chapter 17 : The Canvas of Creativity: Exploring the Dynamic Landscape of AI in Art and Innovation

In the realm of creativity, artificial intelligence (AI) emerges not merely as a tool but as a collaborator, pushing the boundaries of artistic expression and innovation. This article delves into the evolving canvas where human creativity intertwines with the capabilities of AI, creating a dynamic landscape that redefines what is possible.

AI as Co-Creator
In the world of art, AI is transforming from a passive tool to an active co-creator. Artists are harnessing the power of AI algorithms to generate visual masterpieces, compose music, and even craft poetry. This collaboration between human intuition and machine intelligence yields works that challenge preconceived notions of authorship and creativity.

Generative Art
Generative art, born from the fusion of algorithms and artistic intent, exemplifies the synergy between human and machine. AI algorithms, trained on vast datasets, can produce mesmerizing visuals and sculptures. The unpredictability and novelty inherent in generative art mirror the spontaneity of human creativity.

The Harmonic Symphony

In the realm of music, AI's foray into composition is akin to a harmonic symphony. From generating melodies to orchestrating entire pieces, AI algorithms analyze patterns across genres, creating music that resonates with both familiarity and innovation. Musicians are finding inspiration in the collaborative dance with intelligent systems.

Innovation Across Industries

Beyond the arts, AI is a catalyst for innovation across diverse industries. In design, AI assists in creating architectural wonders and fashion ensembles. In healthcare, it aids in drug discovery and medical diagnostics. The canvas of AI creativity extends to business strategy, scientific research, and every facet of human endeavor.

The Ethical Palette

As we explore the creative potential of AI, ethical considerations come to the forefront. Questions of bias in algorithms, accountability in AI-generated content, and the societal impact of automated creativity demand careful contemplation. Balancing innovation with ethical responsibility becomes an integral part of navigating this dynamic canvas.

Educational Brushstrokes

The integration of AI in education opens new possibilities for personalized learning experiences. Intelligent tutoring systems adapt to individual student needs, fostering a collaborative learning environment.

The educational canvas transforms into an ever-evolving landscape tailored to diverse learning styles.

The Future Strokes
Looking ahead, the canvas of AI creativity holds boundless potential. From advancements in natural language processing to the evolution of AI-driven virtual worlds, the future promises a continued interplay between human ingenuity and machine intelligence. Navigating this landscape requires a thoughtful approach that embraces innovation while upholding ethical standards.

The Dance of Algorithms and Aesthetics
In the intersection of algorithms and aesthetics, AI is contributing to the evolution of visual arts. Deep learning algorithms analyze art movements, styles, and color palettes, enabling the creation of artworks that pay homage to historical periods or forge entirely new visual languages. This dance between algorithms and aesthetics blurs the lines between traditional and contemporary art forms.

AI in Cinematic Narratives
The cinematic landscape is undergoing a transformation with AI's influence on storytelling. From script analysis to video editing, AI algorithms assist filmmakers in enhancing narrative coherence, predicting audience preferences, and even generating visual effects. The collaborative nature of AI in film production offers new dimensions to storytelling, challenging filmmakers to explore innovative narrative structures.

Interactive Experiences and Gaming

AI's impact extends to interactive experiences and gaming, where it becomes a dynamic participant in the user's journey. Procedural content generation powered by AI creates ever-changing game environments, adapting to player choices. This not only enhances the gaming experience but also presents a canvas for emergent narratives and unique challenges, providing players with personalized, immersive adventures.

AI-Infused Design Thinking

Design thinking, a human-centered approach to problem-solving, is augmented by AI in the creative process. AI tools assist designers in rapid prototyping, trend analysis, and user feedback interpretation. This collaborative fusion of human intuition and machine-driven insights accelerates the design iteration process, resulting in more innovative and user-centric solutions.

Creative Assistance in Writing

In literature, AI is emerging as a writing companion, offering suggestions for plot twists, character development, and even generating entire paragraphs. Writers collaborate with AI language models, harnessing their linguistic prowess to augment creativity. The synergy between human narrative instincts and AI's linguistic capabilities paints a nuanced picture of storytelling.

AI-Generated Music and Emotional Resonance

AI's role in music composition goes beyond mere melody generation. Algorithms can analyze emotional cues in existing compositions, allowing AI to craft music that resonates with specific moods or evokes particular emotions. The collaborative exploration of emotional resonance in music composition challenges traditional notions of how human emotions are expressed through artistic endeavors.

Cross-Cultural Inspiration
AI acts as a bridge across diverse cultural landscapes, fostering cross-cultural inspiration. By analyzing and interpreting cultural elements from various traditions, AI systems contribute to the creation of artworks that transcend cultural boundaries. This collaborative exchange enriches the global artistic tapestry, fostering a deeper appreciation for cultural diversity.

AI-Driven Personalization in Marketing
In the realm of marketing and advertising, AI algorithms contribute to personalized content creation. By analyzing consumer behaviors and preferences, AI helps tailor marketing campaigns to specific audiences, ensuring that content resonates with individuals on a more personal level. This targeted approach transforms the marketing canvas into a dynamic space that adapts to the diverse tastes of consumers.

AI-Powered Fashion Innovation
Fashion designers are embracing AI to push the boundaries of creativity in the world of apparel. AI algorithms analyze fashion trends, consumer preferences, and historical styles to inspire new designs. Virtual fashion shows and AI-generated designs offer a glimpse into a future where the fusion of technology and

couture transforms the traditional runway into an immersive digital experience.

AI-Enhanced Scientific Discovery

In the scientific realm, AI acts as a catalyst for innovation. From drug discovery to materials science, AI accelerates the research process by analyzing vast datasets, identifying patterns, and predicting outcomes. This collaboration between scientists and AI systems extends the canvas of scientific discovery, opening avenues for breakthroughs that might have been elusive through traditional methods.

AI-Infused Culinary Creativity

The culinary arts experience a renaissance with AI contributing to recipe generation, flavor profiling, and even the creation of entirely new gastronomic experiences. AI-driven algorithms analyze ingredient combinations, nutritional content, and cultural culinary traditions to inspire chefs and home cooks alike. The culinary canvas becomes a fusion of tradition and innovation, inviting experimentation and delighting taste buds.

AI in Architectural Ingenuity

Architects and urban planners leverage AI to reimagine cityscapes and design structures that harmonize with their environments. AI algorithms analyze urban data, climate patterns, and historical architectural styles to inform the creation of sustainable, aesthetically pleasing spaces. The collaborative dance between architects and AI expands the architectural canvas into a realm where form, function, and ecological considerations converge.

AI in Virtual Collaboration Spaces

The rise of virtual collaboration spaces is reshaping how teams create and innovate. AI-powered tools facilitate real-time collaboration, enhancing brainstorming sessions, and providing intelligent insights. Whether in virtual design studios, collaborative coding environments, or digital art platforms, the fusion of human ideation and AI-driven support transforms the collaborative canvas into a dynamic space for collective creation.

AI-Generated Journalism and Storytelling

In journalism and storytelling, AI contributes to content creation and news generation. Automated news articles, AI-driven story suggestions, and natural language generation tools assist journalists in researching and presenting information. This collaborative approach challenges traditional journalistic practices, paving the way for a new era of data-driven, dynamically generated storytelling.

As we continue to explore the multifaceted canvas of creativity enriched by AI, each sector unveils new possibilities and challenges. The collaboration between human ingenuity and artificial intelligence amplifies the potential for innovation, ushering in an era where the boundaries of creativity are continually expanded and redefined.

Bonus Chapter

"AI and Environmental Stewardship: Navigating the Green Horizon"

This bonus chapter delves into the intersection of artificial intelligence and environmental sustainability. It explores how AI technologies can be harnessed to address pressing ecological challenges, ushering in a new era of environmental stewardship.
Climate Modelling and Prediction:
The chapter begins by examining how AI plays a pivotal role in climate modelling and prediction. Readers are introduced to the use of machine learning algorithms to analyse vast datasets, enabling more accurate climate forecasts, assessing environmental risks, and aiding in the development of sustainable practices.

Conservation and Biodiversity

As the narrative unfolds, it explores AI applications in conservation efforts and biodiversity protection. From using drones equipped with AI to monitor endangered species to employing machine learning to analyse ecosystems, readers gain insights into how technology can be a powerful ally in safeguarding the planet's biodiversity.

Sustainable Agriculture and Resource Management

The chapter extends its focus to agriculture and resource management. It delves into how AI-driven precision agriculture optimises crop yields, reduces resource consumption, and contributes to sustainable food production. The narrative also explores the potential of AI in managing water resources and mitigating environmental impact.

Eco-friendly Technologies
Navigating through the green horizon, the chapter introduces readers to eco-friendly technologies powered by AI. From smart grids that enhance energy efficiency to the development of cleaner energy solutions, the narrative showcases how intelligent systems contribute to building a more sustainable and resilient future.

Mindy Questions

Why need of AI and Humans needs collaboration would stable in future ?

The collaboration between humans and AI is essential for several reasons, and it is likely to remain stable and evolve in the future for various compelling factors:

Complementary Strengths
- Humans bring creativity, emotional intelligence, and nuanced decision-making abilities.
- AI excels in processing vast amounts of data, pattern recognition, and executing repetitive tasks with precision.
- The combination of these strengths creates a synergy that enhances overall productivity and problem-solving capabilities.

Enhanced Productivity
- AI can automate routine and time-consuming tasks, allowing humans to focus on higher-order thinking, innovation, and complex problem-solving.
- The collaboration enables a more efficient allocation of resources, leading to increased productivity across various domains.

Innovation and Discovery
- AI technologies, particularly in areas like machine learning and data analysis, can sift through massive datasets to identify patterns, trends, and insights.

- Human creativity is crucial for framing hypotheses, designing experiments, and interpreting results. The collaboration facilitates a more potent exploration of new ideas and scientific discoveries.

Adaptability to Change
- AI can adapt quickly to changes in data and external factors, providing valuable insights and recommendations in real-time.
- Human intuition and critical thinking skills contribute to adapting strategies, navigating ambiguity, and making decisions in complex and dynamic environments.

Human Oversight and Ethical Considerations
- AI systems require human oversight to ensure ethical considerations are addressed, and decisions align with societal values.
- Collaboration with humans helps mitigate the risks of biases in AI algorithms and ensures responsible use of technology.

Customer-Centric Applications
- In customer service and interaction, the combination of AI-driven automation and human empathy creates a more personalized and satisfying experience for users.
- Humans provide the emotional intelligence necessary for understanding complex emotions and unique situations.

Continuous Learning
- Human-AI collaboration fosters a continuous learning environment where humans can adapt and acquire new skills while AI systems learn from human feedback.
- The dynamic interplay between humans and AI contributes to a culture of innovation and adaptability.

As long as the collaboration between humans and AI is approached thoughtfully, with a focus on ethical considerations, transparency, and ongoing learning, it is likely to remain stable and foster a symbiotic relationship that harnesses the unique strengths of both entities. This collaboration has the potential to drive advancements, solve complex challenges, and create a more technologically empowered, yet human-centric, future.

If in case AI run Business and Services , is AI creates job opportunities for Humans ?

Yes, when AI is integrated into businesses and services, it has the potential to create job opportunities for humans in several ways:

AI System Development and Maintenance
- Businesses leveraging AI often require professionals for the development, implementation, and maintenance of AI systems. This includes roles such as AI engineers, machine learning specialists, and data scientists.

AI Training and Oversight
- Humans are needed to train, supervise, and fine-tune AI algorithms. This involves providing guidance, ensuring ethical considerations, and correcting biases that may emerge in AI systems.

User Experience and Interaction
- Roles related to the design of user interfaces, customer service, and user experience become crucial. Humans are better suited to understanding complex emotions, interpreting context, and providing empathetic responses, enhancing the overall user experience.

Data Labeling and Annotation
- Many AI systems require labeled and annotated data for training. Humans play a significant role in data preprocessing, ensuring the quality and accuracy of the datasets used by AI algorithms.

AI Consulting and Implementation
- Professionals who understand both business processes and AI capabilities can provide consulting services to organizations looking to implement AI solutions. This involves assessing needs, recommending solutions, and overseeing the integration of AI into existing workflows.

Ethical and Regulatory Compliance
- With the increased use of AI, there is a growing need for experts in AI ethics, policy, and regulation. Humans are required to navigate the ethical

considerations, ensure responsible AI use, and comply with relevant regulations.

Innovation and Entrepreneurship

- AI-driven businesses often foster innovation and create opportunities for entrepreneurs to establish startups that focus on developing new AI applications or services. This entrepreneurial ecosystem generates job opportunities in various capacities.

Training and Skill Development:

- As businesses adopt AI technologies, there is a demand for training programs and educational initiatives to upskill the workforce. Human instructors and trainers play a vital role in imparting the skills necessary to work alongside AI.

  ◦

While AI can lead to job creation, it's important to acknowledge that the impact on employment depends on various factors, including the industry, the level of AI integration, and the overall economic environment. Proactive measures such as reskilling and upskilling programs, thoughtful workforce planning, and collaboration between industry and educational institutions are crucial for maximizing the positive impact of AI on job opportunities for humans.

Is AI fulfil the Spiritual Purpose?

The question of whether AI can fulfill spiritual. purposes is subjective and depends on one's beliefs, values, and interpretations of spirituality. Here are a few perspectives to consider:

Spirituality and Consciousness
   - Some spiritual perspectives emphasise consciousness, self-awareness, and the interconnectedness of all living things. AI, as of now, lacks true consciousness or self-awareness. It operates based on algorithms and data processing without subjective experiences.

Utilitarian Perspective
   - From a utilitarian standpoint, if AI contributes to the well-being and happiness of individuals or society, it might align with certain spiritual principles. For example, AI applications in healthcare or humanitarian efforts could be seen as contributing to the greater good.

Ethical Considerations
   - The ethical development and use of AI align with spiritual values that emphasize compassion, empathy, and responsible stewardship of resources. Ensuring that AI is developed and deployed ethically can be seen as a spiritual endeavor.

Human-AI Collaboration
  - Some may view the collaboration between humans and AI in a positive light, considering it as a harmonious partnership that combines human creativity, intuition, and ethics with the processing power and efficiency of AI.

Mindful Technology Use
  - Spirituality often encourages mindful and intentional living. Using AI in ways that promote mindfulness, reduce stress, or enhance personal growth could be seen as aligning with spiritual principles.

However, it's essential to acknowledge that AI, as of now, lacks qualities such as consciousness, self-awareness, and intrinsic understanding of spiritual concepts. AI operates based on programmed algorithms and data inputs, devoid of subjective experiences.

The question of whether AI can fulfill spiritual purposes may evolve as technology advances and our understanding of consciousness deepens. As AI continues to develop, it's crucial to approach its integration with careful consideration of ethical, social, and spiritual implications. Ultimately, whether AI aligns with spiritual purposes is a personal and philosophical interpretation that varies among individuals and belief systems.

In Today Times , Human Brain efficiency effected because of easy life Technology?

The impact of technology, including artificial intelligence, on human brain efficiency is a subject of ongoing debate. Here are some perspectives on this matter:

Cognitive Offloading
- Some argue that technology, including AI, has led to cognitive offloading, where individuals rely on external devices and tools to store and retrieve information. This could potentially lead to reduced reliance on memory and critical thinking skills.

Increased Multitasking
- The prevalence of technology, such as smartphones and computers, has led to increased multitasking. Constantly switching between tasks and distractions can affect attention spans and the ability to focus for extended periods.

Information Overload
- The abundance of information available through technology can lead to information overload. Managing vast amounts of data and constant exposure to stimuli might impact cognitive load and decision-making.

Positive Impacts on Learning
- On the positive side, technology, including AI, has enabled new forms of learning and access to

information. Educational apps, online courses, and AI-driven tools can enhance learning experiences and cognitive development.

Concerns about Dependence
- Some express concerns that the ease of access to information through technology might lead to dependence. If individuals become overly reliant on AI for decision-making or problem-solving, it could potentially impact their problem-solving skills.

Technological Facilitation
- Others argue that technology, including AI, can be a tool that facilitates and enhances cognitive abilities. AI systems can assist with complex computations, data analysis, and decision support, freeing up human cognitive resources for more creative and critical thinking tasks.

It's important to note that the impact of technology on the human brain is complex and multifaceted. The relationship between AI and human cognitive efficiency can vary based on factors such as how individuals use technology, the nature of their work, and the balance between technology dependence and empowerment.

Ultimately, the effects of technology on the human brain are nuanced, and ongoing research in psychology, neuroscience, and human-computer interaction is essential to understand these dynamics better. It's crucial for individuals to be mindful of their technology use and strike a balance that enhances cognitive abilities without sacrificing essential skills.

While artificial intelligence (AI) brings about numerous benefits, it also raises concerns and potential negative impacts. Here are some key areas where AI can have negative consequences:

Job Displacement

- Automation and AI technologies can lead to job displacement in certain industries. Tasks that can be automated may result in reduced demand for certain roles, potentially leading to unemployment for some workers.

Bias and Discrimination

- AI systems may inadvertently perpetuate or even exacerbate existing biases present in the data they are trained on. This can result in discriminatory outcomes, affecting decisions in areas like hiring, lending, and law enforcement.

Loss of Privacy

- The extensive collection and analysis of data by AI systems raise privacy concerns. Surveillance technologies, data mining, and profiling can compromise individual privacy rights, leading to a loss of personal autonomy.

Security Risks

- AI systems are susceptible to adversarial attacks, where malicious actors manipulate inputs to deceive the system. Security vulnerabilities in AI technologies can be exploited for unauthorized access, fraud, or other malicious activities.

Ethical Considerations
- AI raises complex ethical questions, such as the development of autonomous weapons, the potential misuse of AI in influencing public opinion, and the moral implications of decisions made by AI systems, especially in critical areas like healthcare and criminal justice.

Dependency and Reliability
- Overreliance on AI systems, especially in critical domains, can be risky. System failures, errors, or unexpected behaviors can have significant consequences, and humans may become overly dependent on technology without fully understanding its limitations.

Social Inequality
- Access to and benefits from AI technologies may not be distributed equally. There is a risk of exacerbating social inequalities, as those with limited access to technology or the skills needed to leverage it may be left behind.

Lack of Accountability
- Determining responsibility for decisions made by AI systems can be challenging. Lack of transparency and accountability in AI algorithms can lead to difficulty in addressing errors, biases, or unintended consequences.

It's crucial to address these negative impacts proactively through ethical AI development, responsible deployment, and the establishment of robust regulatory frameworks. As AI continues to advance, society must navigate these challenges to ensure that the benefits of AI are realized without compromising fundamental values and well-being.

As we conclude this exploration into the transformative landscape of artificial intelligence in "Rise of Artificial Intelligence Mind," the journey has been both enlightening and thought-provoking. The rise of AI marks a pivotal epoch in human history, one where the synergy between machine intelligence and human ingenuity shapes the very fabric of our existence. As we navigate the possibilities and challenges on this horizon, may this book serve as a guide, igniting discussions, sparking innovations, and fostering a collective mindfulness in steering the course of AI toward a future where technology elevates the human experience. The future awaits, and with it, the unfolding chapters of a world shaped by the burgeoning power of artificial intelligence.Bonus Tip , Everything you still read all Data written by An Raise of Brain. Hope you enjoyed the Realm of AI , that's the power of Artificial Intelligence.

www.ingramcontent.com/pod-product-compliance
Lightning Source LLC
LaVergne TN
LVHW041220050326
832903LV00021B/713